11141

796.1
Downer, Marion

Kites

DATE DUE			

KITES

HOW TO MAKE
AND FLY THEM

KITES
HOW TO MAKE
AND FLY THEM

BY MARION DOWNER

LOTHROP, LEE AND SHEPARD CO.
NEW YORK

To Earl Oliver Hurst
whose wish was
that boys and girls
the world over
share in the fun
of making and flying
their own kites.

Eighth printing, October 1971

CONTENTS

YOUR HAND-MADE KITE

You will understand all kites better when you make your own—their strength, their balance and their performance in the air. It is easy to buy a kite. But any ready-made kite will be just like a thousand others and does not stand a chance if it competes in a contest.

You will like the string, the new sticks and the smell of glue when you are building a certain kind of kite you have in mind. And there are so many different kinds to try. They look different and they fly differently. A large kite takes less wind than a small one and some of them go up as high as two miles.

Find the possibilities and the flaws in your own hand-made kites. This is the air age. Try out the skies.

TOOLS needed for kite making

A sharp knife

Scissors

A ruler and a yardstick

A small saw

A pencil

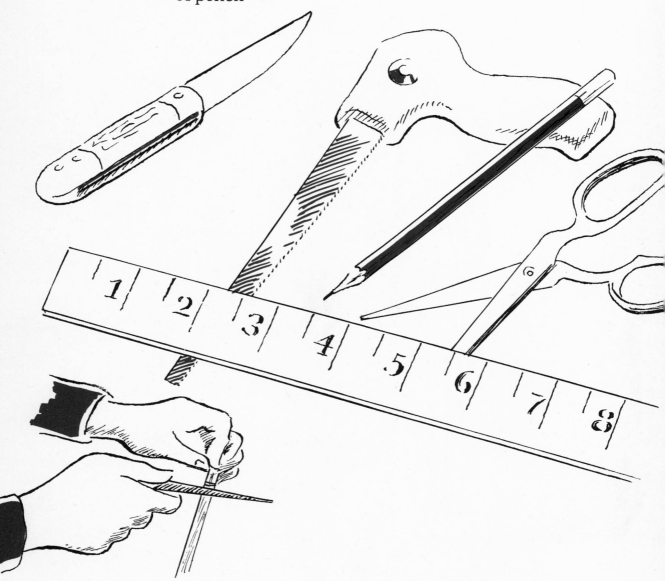

MATERIALS used in kite making

It is always fun to take whatever is handy and make something out of it. Boys used to climb trees and cut twigs to make kite frames. They covered the frames with newspaper or cheesecloth. Of course the twigs were seldom straight enough, the newspaper tore easily, the cheesecloth let the air go through it, but the kites flew for a while.

Here are materials that are more serviceable:

STICKS: Lumber yards will cut spruce, pine or cedar into strips ⅜, ½ or ¾ of an inch wide. Forty inches is a good length for the kites shown in this book. Sometimes a mill has just what you want in its discard pile. Dowel sticks are sold for a few cents at hardware stores. They are round and strong and come in several widths, 36 inches long.

STRING: Fish line is strong and inexpensive. Good cotton or hemp twine will serve most purposes.

PAPER: Gift-wrapping paper for color, white butcher's paper for greatest strength. Charcoal drawing paper comes in good shades but is not very light. Tissue paper from an Oriental crafts shop is perfect kite paper.

CLOTH: Glazed cotton has good resistance to air currents. Rayon is strong and light. Nylon is tough and has little weight. Most plastics are either too heavy or too fragile.

ADHESIVES: For the folded borders of the coverings (cloth or paper) use flour paste or rubber cement. Joinings on the wood frame need glue, which must be dried over night, or quick-drying cement.

YOUR WORK SPACE

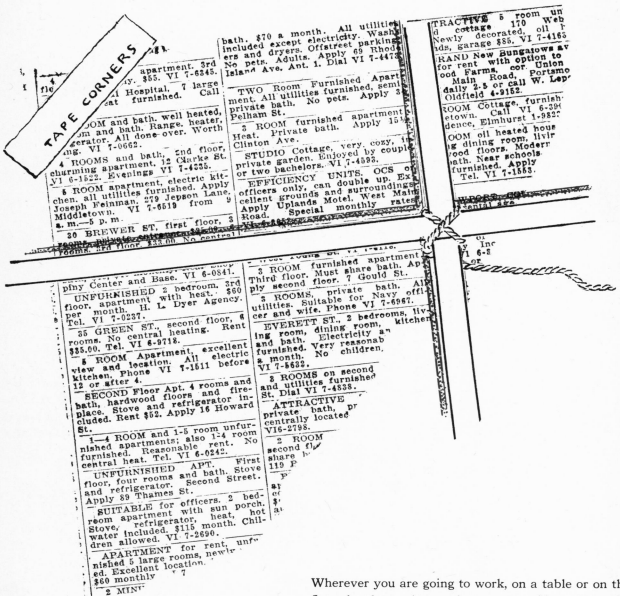

Wherever you are going to work, on a table or on the floor, lay large sheets of newspaper. Tape down the corners.

This sketch shows how to lay sticks at **RIGHT ANGLES.**

Use your yardstick to draw colored pencil lines on the newspaper, up and down, and across where the printed words and lines go. Lay the sticks you want to tie, on the colored pencil lines and your kite sticks will be at right angles.

EXTRA HELPS

Small patches of masking tape will keep sticks in place while you tie them.

When you have to punch holes in your kite covering, protect the holes with round cloth patches.

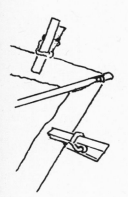

Use pinch clothespins to hold folds of covering before or after pasting.

Colored crayons are useful to make marks easily seen on wood, paper, cloth and even on twine.

CONSTRUCTION METHODS

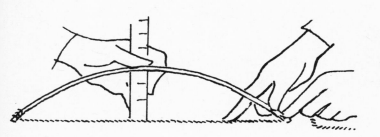

Place a crayon mark on the middle of your bow stick. Then soak bow stick in water so it will bend without breaking. Tie cord to one end and pull until bow is at the right height.

Make saw-cuts in ends of sticks. Fill them with glue, then shove cord into slots when making kite outlines.

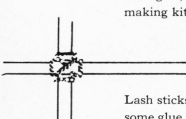

Lash sticks where they cross and spread on some glue to keep strings from slipping.

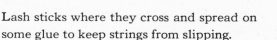

Where large sticks cross, whittle or file slight cutouts so sticks lie flatter.

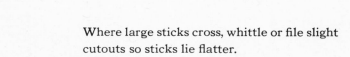

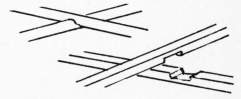

REELS

When you fly your kite you will need a reel to wind up and let out cord without getting it into tangles.

Contest kite flyers often have a kind of reel that spins mechanically, but some of them use only a short stick with hand-hold space at each end.

Most reels have guards to keep the cord between them and can be made by any home carpenter. Painted or stained, they are good-looking tools.

A day when you have to wait for fair weather and a kite breeze is a good time to make a reel.

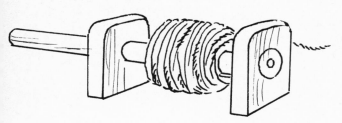

Guards made out of board—sawed, whittled and sanded—are set onto a piece of broomstick.

A very simple reel is cut in the shape of a flat paddle out of a 5-inch board.

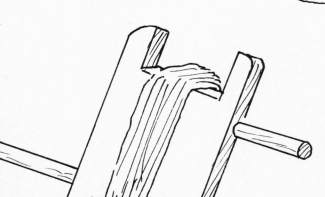

To make this reel use a board ¾ of an inch thick. Saw it so there is a winding space with projecting guards. Bore holes in the sides and insert pieces of pole or dowel sticks for hand-holds.

BRIDLES

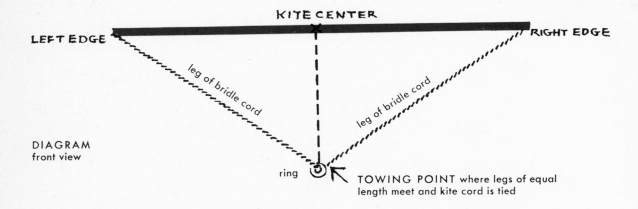

LEFT EDGE

KITE CENTER

RIGHT EDGE

leg of bridle cord

leg of bridle cord

DIAGRAM
front view

ring

TOWING POINT where legs of equal
length meet and kite cord is tied

Bridles are the cords attached to the kite sticks and leading to the flying cord. They are centered from side to side.

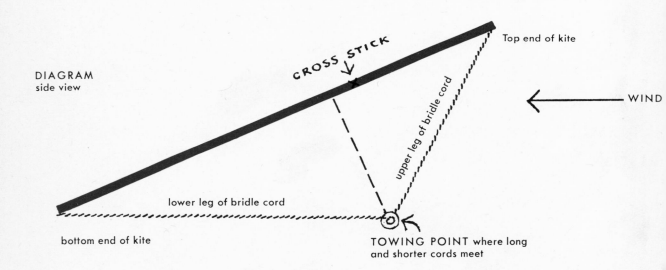

DIAGRAM
side view

CROSS STICK

Top end of kite

WIND

upper leg of bridle cord

lower leg of bridle cord

bottom end of kite

TOWING POINT where long
and shorter cords meet

The bridle cord that goes from end to end must tilt the kite's nose upward to catch the wind beneath, so the top cord is made shorter. Both cords meet just below the place where the cross stick is tied to the upright.

14

TAILS and a PARACHUTE

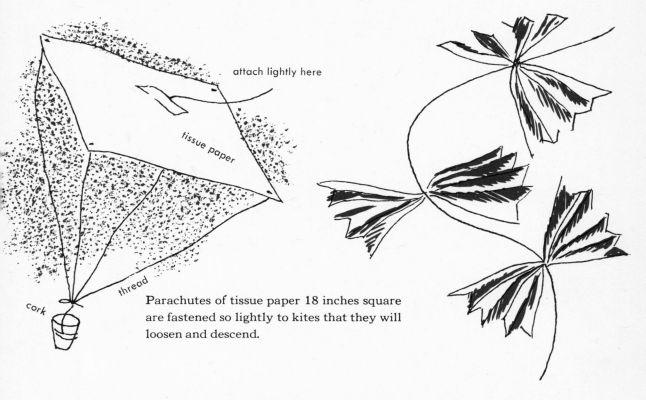

attach lightly here

tissue paper

thread

cork

Parachutes of tissue paper 18 inches square are fastened so lightly to kites that they will loosen and descend.

A tail helps to balance a kite that might tip and spin without one. It is not the weight but the waving of the tail, crosswise to the breeze, that gives balance.

A rag tail is good, if it is not too heavy. Tissue paper on a thread is lighter and swishes more easily.

A neat and decorative way to make kite tails is to cut tissue paper in pieces 6 x 4 inches. Fold lengthwise three or four times, then tie a string around each center. Spread the ends in fan-shape and tie them 8 inches apart along 30 feet of thread.

Take an extra supply of kite tail to the flying field. Wrap it around a carton to keep it from tangling.

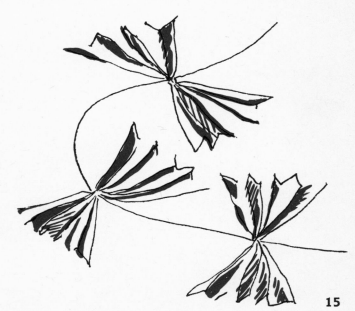

KITES TO MAKE

FLAT KITES

Flat kites are the easiest kind to make. The size shown here, three feet long, is sometimes doubled or tripled in the same proportions. An experiment has been tried of making one 8 feet long, covering it with racing duck and giving it a flying cord of mackerel line. Flown from the prow of a dory, it sails the boat.

MATERIALS: 1 stick 36 inches long (the upright, or mast stick).
1 stick 30 inches long (the cross stick, or spar).
1 square yard of cloth or paper.

DIRECTIONS: Make a crayon mark at the center of the 30-inch cross stick. Lay it at right angles across the upright, 9 inches down from the top. Glue and lash the sticks together. Make saw cuts crosswise in ends of all four sticks. Run string around from tip to tip and tie. Lay this frame on your covering.

FRAME
with string outlines.

Cut covering to this shape, leaving margins of at least 2 inches all around.

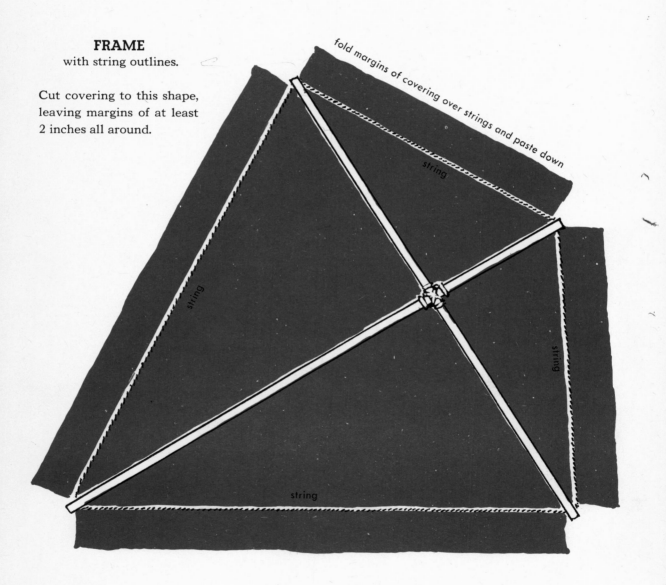

fold margins of covering over strings and paste down

string

string

string

string

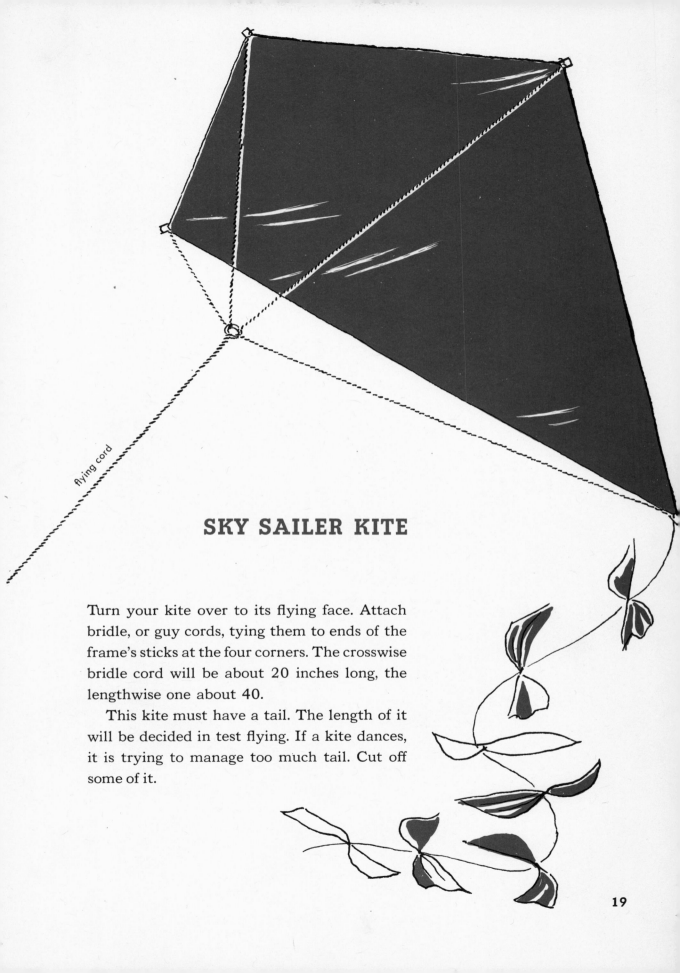

flying cord

SKY SAILER KITE

Turn your kite over to its flying face. Attach bridle, or guy cords, tying them to ends of the frame's sticks at the four corners. The crosswise bridle cord will be about 20 inches long, the lengthwise one about 40.

This kite must have a tail. The length of it will be decided in test flying. If a kite dances, it is trying to manage too much tail. Cut off some of it.

19

MATERIALS: 1 slender, bendable stick 30 inches long (the bow).
1 stronger stick ⅜ or ½ inch wide, 36 inches long (the arrow).
Cloth or paper 36 x 42 inches.

DIRECTIONS: Cut or file a notch in the top end of the 36-inch stick. Cut a groove for string just below the notch. Then make a saw cut into the bottom end of the stick.

Make a crayon mark at the exact center of the slender bow stick and fit that center into the notch with glue. Be sure the sticks are at right angles and tie them firmly where they cross.

Measure two yards of string. Fill the saw cut at bottom with glue and slip the exact center of the string into it. Let this frame, with string hanging loose, dry spread out flat.

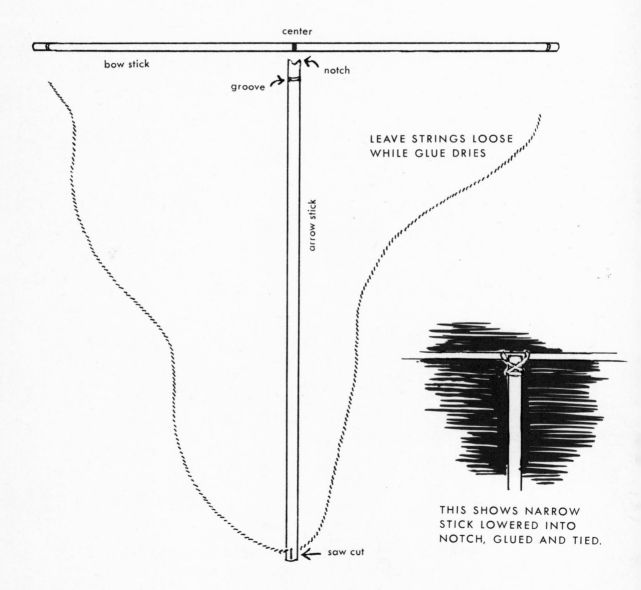

center

bow stick

groove

notch

LEAVE STRINGS LOOSE
WHILE GLUE DRIES

arrow stick

saw cut

THIS SHOWS NARROW
STICK LOWERED INTO
NOTCH, GLUED AND TIED.

ARCHED-TOP KITE

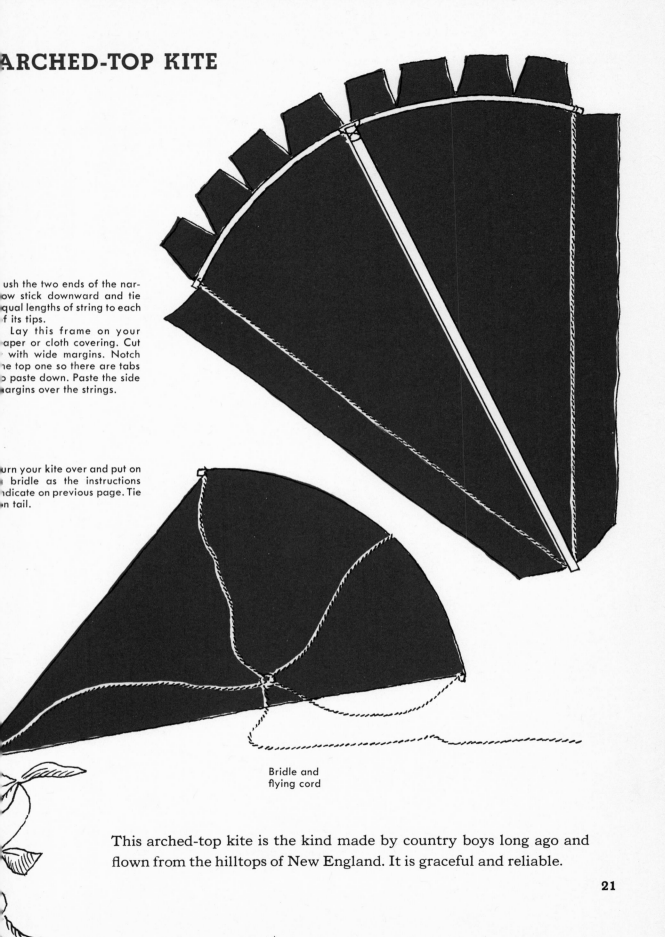

...ush the two ends of the nar-
...ow stick downward and tie
...qual lengths of string to each
...f its tips.

Lay this frame on your
...aper or cloth covering. Cut
... with wide margins. Notch
...e top one so there are tabs
...o paste down. Paste the side
...argins over the strings.

...urn your kite over and put on
... bridle as the instructions
...ndicate on previous page. Tie
...n tail.

Bridle and
flying cord

This arched-top kite is the kind made by country boys long ago and
flown from the hilltops of New England. It is graceful and reliable.

MATERIALS: 2 dowel sticks ⅛ inch diameter, 24 inches long (the x sticks).
1 dowel stick ⅛ inch diameter, 18 inches long (the cross stick).
1 thin, flat stick 6 inches long (brace).
1 thin, flat stick 8 inches long (brace).
String for edges of frame, 7 feet long.
Paper 24 inches square.

DIRECTIONS: Make marks on each of the 24-inch sticks, 10 inches from their top ends. Cross them at that place, having the top ends 10½ inches apart. Lay the 18-inch stick horizontally across with its exact center on top of the crossing point, and lash the three together firmly.

Measure 3 inches down from crossing point and lay the 6-inch brace across. Measure 6 inches down and lay the 8-inch brace. Glue and tie them. Lay the frame on your covering. Cut a round hole between the two short sticks.

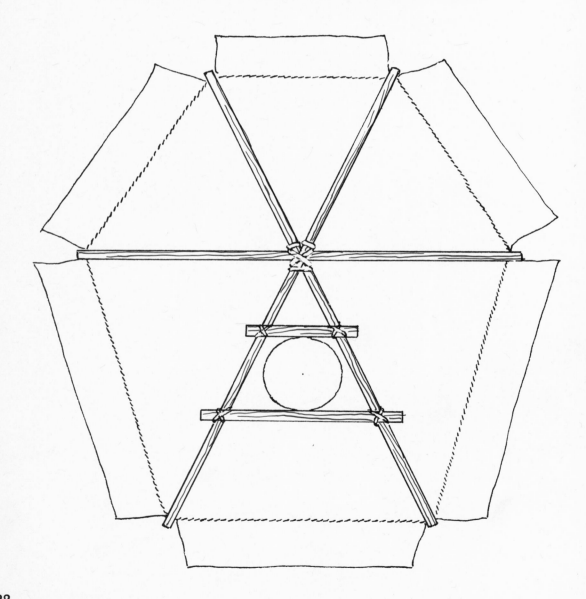

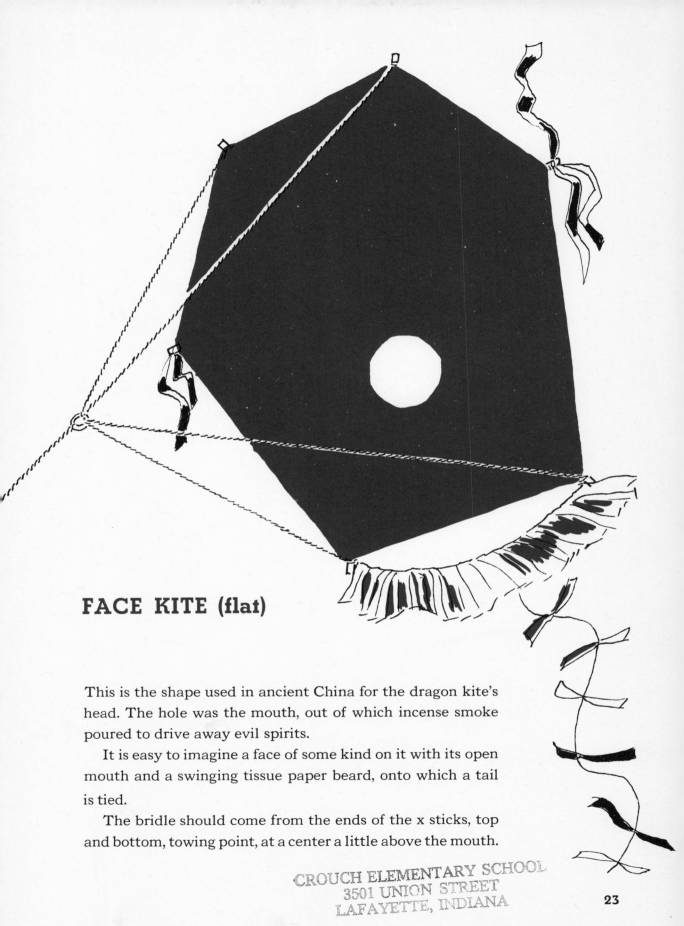

FACE KITE (flat)

This is the shape used in ancient China for the dragon kite's head. The hole was the mouth, out of which incense smoke poured to drive away evil spirits.

It is easy to imagine a face of some kind on it with its open mouth and a swinging tissue paper beard, onto which a tail is tied.

The bridle should come from the ends of the x sticks, top and bottom, towing point, at a center a little above the mouth.

MATERIALS: 1 light, bendable stick 40 inches long.
2 dowel sticks 3/16 inch diameter, 26 inches long.
1 round or square stick about 3/16 inch wide, 10 inches long.
Cloth or paper 30 x 40 inches.

DIRECTIONS: Take the two 26-inch sticks that are to meet at top and form the bird's bill. Whittle off their inner sides for half an inch so when pressed together they will make a slender point. Make a mark on each of these sticks 18 inches down. There tie the 10-inch stick as a brace and glue the bill points together. The tail ends of the sticks will be 14 inches apart.

Tie a string to each end of the 40-inch stick. Do not bend it yet. Tie its central part across the bill end 5 inches down from bill point at each side. Now draw the strings and tie them, one to each end of the cross brace stick, each string measuring 15 inches from wing tip. String the tail separately from lower tips and across to ends of brace stick. Lay frame on covering.

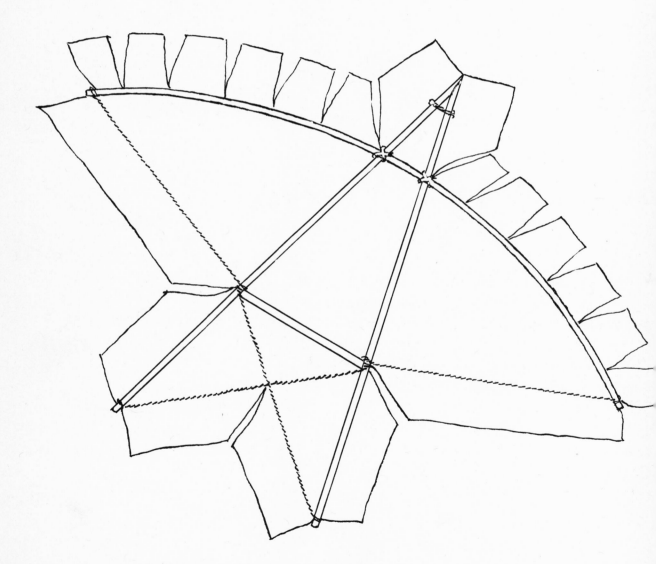

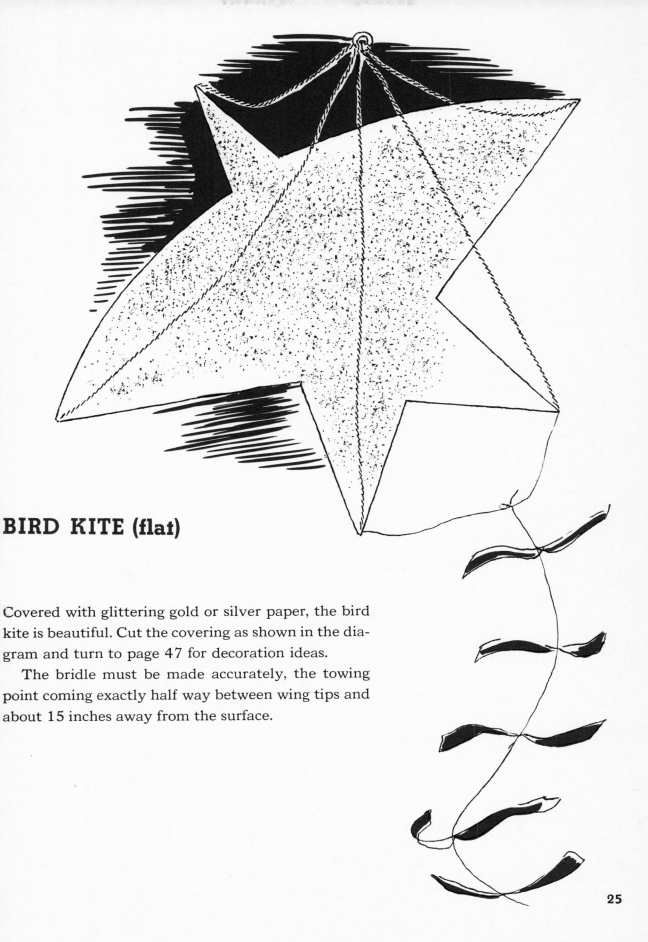

BIRD KITE (flat)

Covered with glittering gold or silver paper, the bird kite is beautiful. Cut the covering as shown in the diagram and turn to page 47 for decoration ideas.

The bridle must be made accurately, the towing point coming exactly half way between wing tips and about 15 inches away from the surface.

BOW KITES

Kites with curved-out fronts were introduced in America by William Eddy who copied them after the native Malay kite. They are now made with various outline shapes and with one or more bows to curve their surfaces from side to side.

Tailless bow kites have remarkable balance. A breeze, pressing against one half, gives a force that buoys up the other half.

MATERIALS: 1 strong stick 36 inches long (mast or spine stick).
1 bendable stick 34 inches long (bow stick).
Covering 38 x 40 inches. Cloth is best for a bow kite.

DIRECTIONS: Put a crayon mark at center of bow stick. Tie a string to one end. Draw it until the bow bends and the string is 28 inches long between ends. The bow will then be bent to a depth of 5½ inches at its center. Put a crayon mark at the center of that bow string. Lay the bow down. Cross the spine stick over it at right angles to bow string and at its center, 7 inches from top. String the outer edges and lay the frame on your cloth.

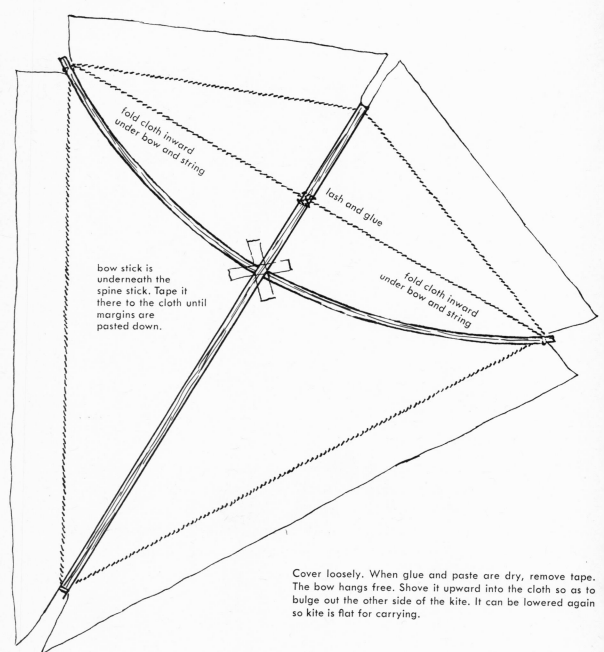

fold cloth inward under bow and string

lash and glue

bow stick is underneath the spine stick. Tape it there to the cloth until margins are pasted down.

fold cloth inward under bow and string

Cover loosely. When glue and paste are dry, remove tape. The bow hangs free. Shove it upward into the cloth so as to bulge out the other side of the kite. It can be lowered again so kite is flat for carrying.

EDDY BOW KITE (tailless)

Experts consider this kite the world's most trustworthy flyer.

It can be flown by a single cord coming from the center of the bow. But with a bridle from top and bottom ends it will be more easily managed. The towing point must be a little lower than the curve of the bow. No tail is needed.

MATERIALS: 1 stick ¾ or ½ inch wide, 36 inches long (mast or spine stick).
2 light, bendable sticks each 36 inches long (bows).
Covering 40 x 40 inches. Cloth is best.

DIRECTIONS: Make crayon marks at the centers of both bow sticks. Tie a string to an end of each and pull until the bow bends and the strings measure 33 inches after tying. Lay these two bows down with their strings parallel and 12 inches apart. Lay the mast stick across at right angles to strings and fasten the strings only to the mast. Lay this frame on the cloth and tape it while you string the outline and fold the borders down.

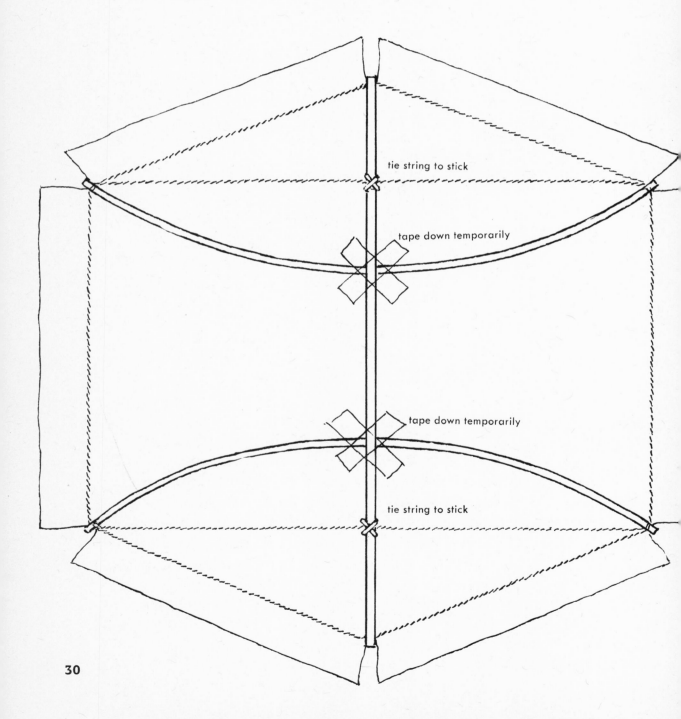

tie string to stick

tape down temporarily

tape down temporarily

tie string to stick

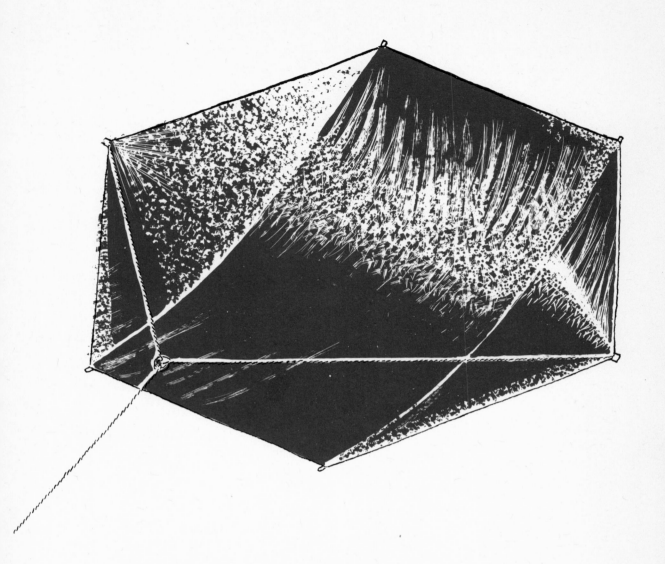

DOUBLE BOW KITE (tailless)

Push the two bows into the covering and the face of the kite will have a wide curving spread left and right. The point at the top of the mast stick is in the lead when flying.

From each tip of the mast stick a two-leg bridle is attached. The towing point is above center, so that the lower part is longer than the upper one, raising the nose of the kite against the breeze.

MATERIALS: 2 dowel sticks, ¼ inch width, 36 inches long (x).
1 lighter, bendable stick, 36 inches long (bow).
Covering 30 x 38 inches. Cloth is best.

DIRECTIONS: Make a crayon mark on each of the two x sticks 10½ inches from top ends. Cross them there with the lower ends spread 19 inches apart. Glue and tie them in that position. While they dry tie a string to one end of the bow stick. Pull the string toward the other end and tie it there when the string is tight enough to measure 26 inches between knots.

Place the x stick on top of the bow and string. Tie the exact center of the string to the crossing of the x sticks. String at the six corners and push bow forward into the cloth.

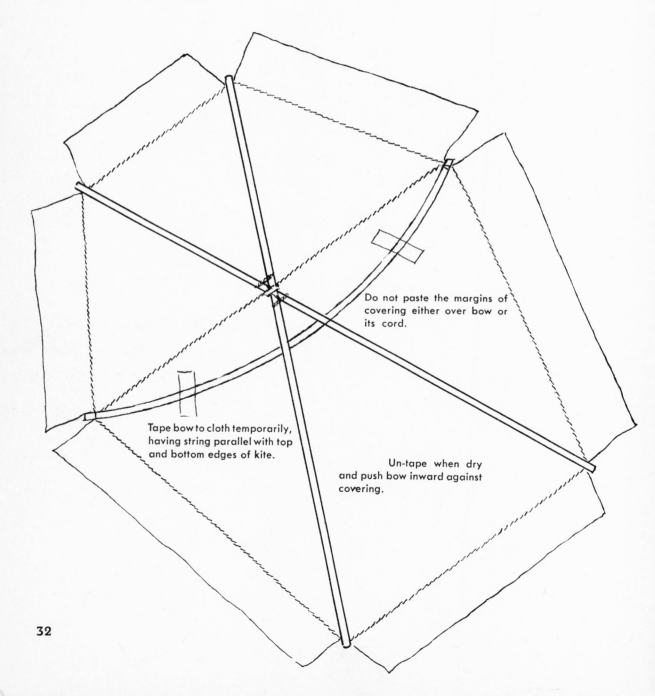

Do not paste the margins of covering either over bow or its cord.

Tape bow to cloth temporarily, having string parallel with top and bottom edges of kite.

Un-tape when dry and push bow inward against covering.

FLAT-NOSE BOW KITE (tailless)

This kite's flat nose is narrow and it fans out-
ward to the curve of the bow in a way that gives
lift against the breeze. The towing point of the
bridle must come a little below the bow and be
absolutely centered, right and left.

BOX KITES

Box kites are three-dimensional. They have boxes or cells to capture the wind. Sometimes they are made in very complex designs with many cells for extra lift. Their inventor, Lawrence Hargrave of England, made one that could carry a man aloft.

Box kites of one type are in use in the United States Air Force. They are provided on life rafts for the purpose of raising antennae on emergency radios.

MATERIALS: 4 sticks ⅜ inch square, 36 inches long (uprights).

8 sticks ⅜ inch square, 11 inches long (box frames).

4 sticks ⅜ inch square, 15½ inches long (braces).

1 cloth or paper strip, 13 inches wide ⎫

1 cloth or paper strip, 15 inches wide ⎬ 48 inches long

DIRECTIONS: Build two square frames out of the 11-inch sticks for the box ends of the kite. Stand the four uprights into the corners of these frames, one at top and one at bottom. Place the braces inside from corner to corner at the middle of the top and bottom boxes. Notch their ends to fit tightly against uprights, shortening them if necessary, and glue.

Make crayon marks on the uprights, 9 inches down from top and 11 inches up from bottom edge. Run string around the four sides at those marks. Put covering on the two boxes.

Lay the frame on the floor and cover with strips of paper, cut 4 inches wider than the boxes. Slash the corners and paste in the 2-inch margins.

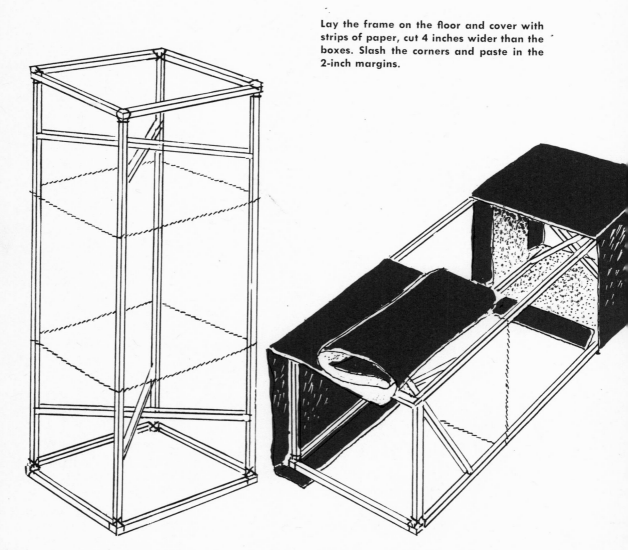

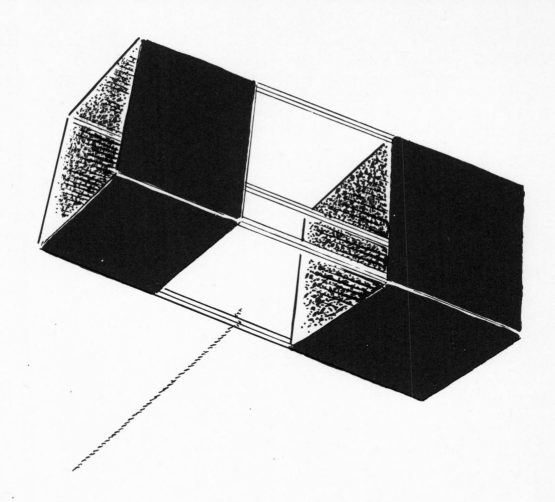

SQUARE-END BOX KITE

This kite flies steadily when one corner edge is
downward and the breeze lifts equally against
two flat sides. At the same time the upper
angles of the boxes are filled with air passing
through.

No bridle is needed, nor any tail. Fasten your
flying cord at the middle of the stick between
the two boxes.

MATERIALS: 4 sticks 3/16 inch wide, 36 inches long (uprights).
4 sticks 3/16 inch wide, 24 inches long (frame sides).
4 sticks 3/16 inch wide, 7 inches long (frame ends).
2 sticks ¼ inch wide, 24¼ inches long (braces).
Wrapping paper, brown 48 x 40 inches or white 3 yards.

DIRECTIONS: Build the frame of the four-sided structure by standing the upright sticks, tying and gluing their ends to the frame side sticks. Then join these sides by tying in the short frame end sticks, making a tall box. Half way down the upright sticks, make crayon marks and fit in the braces from corner to corner. Run string around the frame in two places, 9 inches down from top and 19 inches up from bottom. Cover boxes between sticks and strings. Leave ends open.

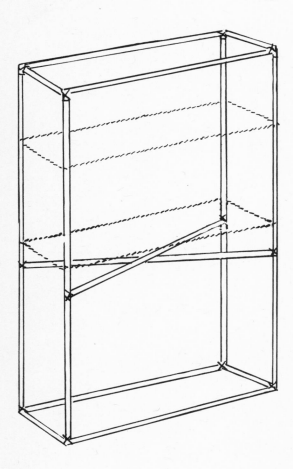

Paste margins under string.

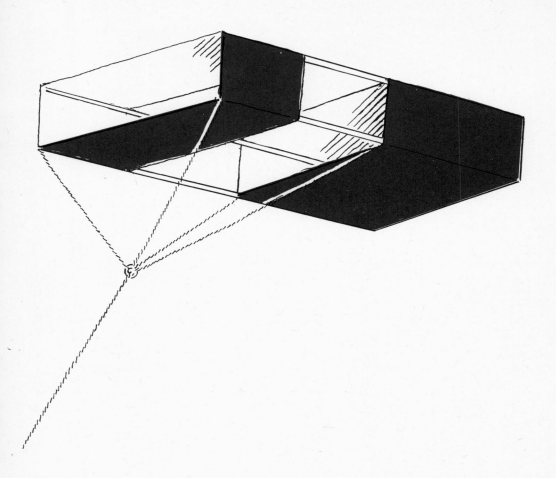

OBLONG-END BOX KITE

The biplane flown by the Wright Brothers was like this kite in general appearance. It floats on one wide, flat side with a bridle coming from the top corners of each box. The towing point is just beneath the lower edge of the upper box.

MATERIALS: 2 sticks ½ inch square, 30 inches long (uprights, front).
2 sticks ½ inch square, 31½ inches long (uprights, rear).
2 sticks ⅜ inch wide, 18 inches long (base, front and back).
2 sticks ⅜ inch wide, 13½ inches long (base ends).
1 dowel stick ¼ inch width, 18 inches long (top edge at angle).
1 flat stick 17¼ inches long (cross brace at front).
2 flat sticks 27¾ inches long (slanting braces at front).
Cloth covering, 2 yards.

DIRECTIONS: Build an oblong frame out of the four base sticks, making sure that the corners of it are right angles. Tie and glue the 30 inch uprights into the front corners of this oblong base and the 31½ inch uprights into its rear corners. Tie the top ends of the uprights together, two left and two right. Across their points, glue the ¼ inch round dowel stick. Put on front cross brace 9 inches down from top. Fit the slant braces from center of base at front to corners at cross brace.

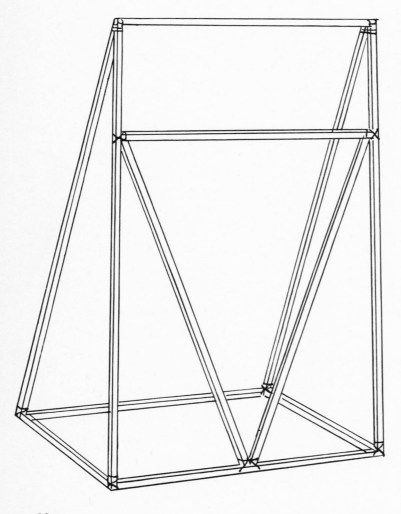

Put covering over top of front and down over back. Cover the two triangles, left and right. Leave sides, bottom, and triangle at center front, open.

FLYING WEDGE KITE

This type of box kite is in the strongest puller class. The value of the wedge shape is in the peaked top, where the wind, coming in from bottom and sides, is trapped and drives the kite by its force.

The bridle comes from the three corners of the open center and is centered right and left. The cords should be strong ones.

MATERIALS:　2 sticks ½ inch width, 37½ inches long (triangle sides).

1 stick ½ inch width, 34 inches long (cross beam).

1 stick ½ inch width, 37½ inches long (triangle ridge).

6 sticks ½ inch width, 12 inches long (triangle supports).

Covering for triangle part, 2 strips 18 and 16 inches wide by four feet long; for each wing, a strip 16 inches wide by 40 inches.

DIRECTIONS:　Lay down two of the 37½ inch sticks, parallel and 12 inches apart. Glue and tie the 34-inch cross beam at right angles, 12 inches from top. Build the triangular roof-like section with the other 37½ inch stick for top ridge and the six 12-inch sticks as pairs of supports, placed 6 inches from each end. Lower this roof frame onto the two parallel sticks. Let their cross pieces come exactly 6 inches from each end of kite frame. Glue and tie there.

String around all stick ends, triangles included. Also run string around the triangle 12 inches from top ends and 14 inches from bottom ends. Boxes are now outlined by string. Cover as shown.

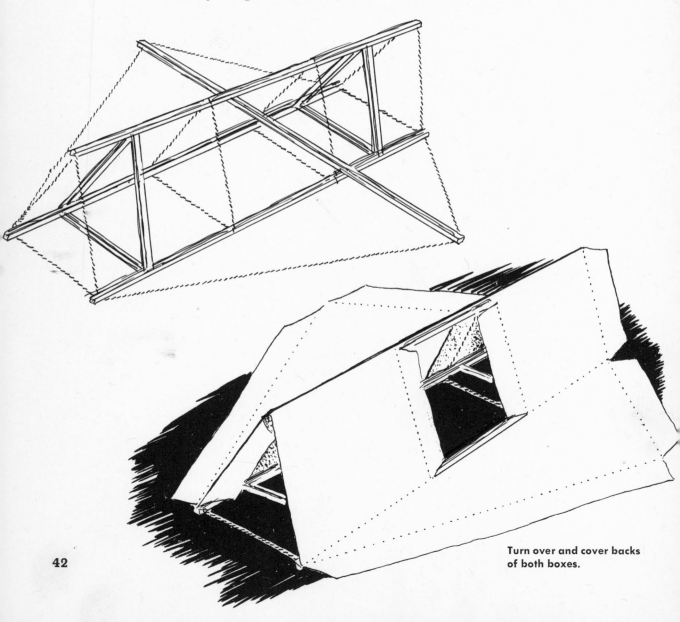

Turn over and cover backs of both boxes.

42

flying cord

TRIANGULAR BOX KITE (with wings)

The top is flat, with the cross beam spreading from tip to tip of the wings. The bottom edge of the kite is the apex, or ridge, of the triangular tunnel. It flies in balance with a single cord tied there near the smaller box.

This kite is geometrically beautiful and a swift climber.

KITE COLORING

Your kite may be a very good flyer, even though made of ordinary wrapping paper, and with no other ornament than your name carefully lettered.

But if you have time, think of color and decoration. Imagine how it will look at a distance in the sky. An unusual color will help you keep watch of your own kite among many others flying near it.

COLORS

The shapes of kites are beautiful. They have potential grace. Even the bare frames are interesting structurally.

But their colors can be especially fascinating—silver like the moon, orange of a sunset, pink as the dawn, purple for a thunder cloud, deep blue of the sea, white of a snowcap, green for an iceberg, gold as a guiding star, yellow of a comet's tail.

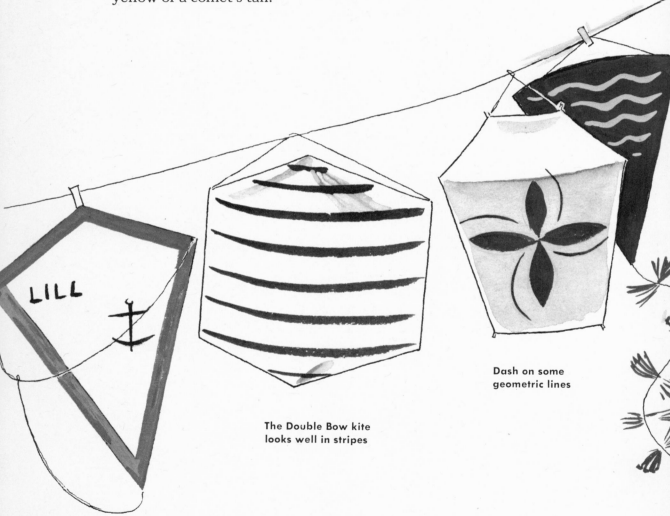

Dash on some
geometric lines

The Double Bow kite
looks well in stripes

Name your kite, either for fun or for sentiment.
Like boats, kites are usually given feminine names.

CAUTION: Don't be too ambitious with decorations that may increase the weight of your kite.

Give your Bird kite some brush
strokes for plumage.

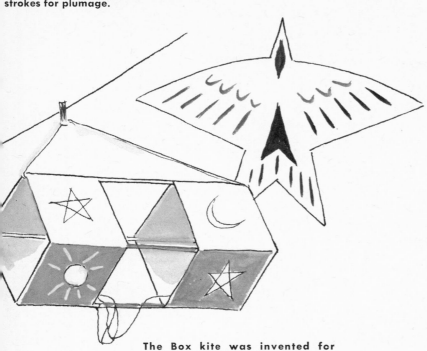

The Box kite was invented for
weather observations. Draw sky sym-
bols on it.

The Oblong Box kite stands decora-
tively on a table. Paste or draw a
ship on its flat panels.

DECORATIONS

Think of decorations that will be pleasing when your
kite is in your hands and especially when it is hanging
by its bridle cords on your wall or from your ceiling.

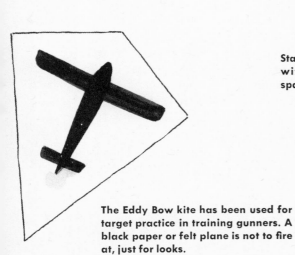

Start making circles on a Face kite
with a compass. Soon there are
spaces to fill in with paint.

The Eddy Bow kite has been used for
target practice in training gunners. A
black paper or felt plane is not to fire
at, just for looks.

YOUR KITE IN THE SKY

If you have flown a kite, you already know how. If you haven't you can learn a lot about it from the directions here and from watching other kite flyers.

Flight theory has fascinated people ever since the first kite was sent up. Kite flying has given knowledge and pleasure, and has had its practical uses. Lives at sea were saved long ago with lifelines flown out to stranded ships by kites.

And who knows what discoveries your kite in the sky may make for you?

TO LAUNCH

The best kite breeze is from eight to fifteen miles per hour. It will extend a small flag or a handkerchief held by the corners in your hand. An eighteen-mile wind will toss the treetops. That is too strong for most kites. Extra sturdy ones are safe in a twenty-mile wind, but they must be specially built if they are to battle higher ones.

A kite ready to launch is a tilted plane. Under the best conditions you need not even give it a boost, but offer it from your hand until a puff of wind makes it mount. A Malay can lie with its curved side to the ground, and catch a breeze to lift it.

But if you have someone to act as a starter, stand with your own back to the wind, holding the reel. Let out fifty or seventy-five feet of string loosely, but not touching the ground. The starter, with the wind blowing toward him, holds the kite from the rear at the cross sticks, and tilts it slightly upward, judging an angle that will let the breeze flow underneath. The tail should be spread in front of him.

As soon as the starter feels a steady pull on the line from the reel in your hands, the wind is pressing against the kite. Give him a signal to "cast off." Then he must let go of the kite, without tossing it. As it rises, let out string, but you should never have to run.

YOUR KITE IN THE SKY

It balances on a pivot from tip to tip. Its center line tugs at the taut string in your hand.

The air pressure is equal to the wind velocity. Like a plane, a kite rises into the vacuum it creates above its upper side. It will float static for hours when pressure from above and below are equal.

TO FLY

Up in the air your kite may meet with strong and shifting winds. A good kite will do its best to steady itself by maintaining the balance angle, but it will wobble, spin or dive if the wind force against its two halves is unequal. This unbalance may be due to a defect in the kite. Either it has one side heavier than the other or the bridle cord is not centered. If the kite resists rising, and sags downward, the tail is too heavy. Cut off a foot or two.

A new kite may have to be brought down several times for corrections. To bring a kite down, walk or run *with* the wind, toward the kite, and reel in as you run, maneuvering to avoid a landing on trees or rooftops. It takes several minutes.

To correct defective balance see that the bridle is the same length side to side. See that there is no tear in the cover on one side, so that air pressure is being lost by leakage. Make sure the sticks have not loosened, are not slipping out of place. Lop off some tail if lightness is needed.

Up again, walk backward, giving short jerks on the line, without reeling in. This will often give a kite more lift. Each tug can make it climb a little higher.

Spinning or diving can sometimes be stopped by suddenly letting out several more feet of line and giving your kite freedom to rise into a more favorable wind.

Air currents change and give you sudden problems. Air pressure that strikes at an angle is deflected at the same angle but its force comes halfway between.

SAFETY OBSERVANCES

Do not run across highways when flying kites.

Do not climb to dangerous heights to retrieve a kite that is caught.

Do not throw rocks at electric wires to loosen a kite hanging from them.

Keep your cord dry. Electricity, from power wires or from lightning, will pass through a wet cord faster than through the surrounding air. Never use a wire kite line.

Safe space for kite flying is reserved in city parks and playgrounds. An open field is the best place but a wide beach is excellent.

KITE FLYING CONTESTS

It is fun to fly your kite alone where all the sky is your own. But sometimes you will like company and competition.

Perhaps there is a kite club in your community. They are organized to put on contests or tournaments with managers and judges. They announce the day, the place, the rules and what you must do to enter your kite and fly it with many others.

Winning or losing, it is fun.

ENTERING YOUR KITE

(Quoted by permission of National Recreation
Association from their publication *Flying High.*)

CLASSIFICATION OF KITES

Kites are usually divided into three groups:

1. Plane surface kites, or those having tails

2. Bow or tailless kites

3. Box kites or combination kites. Tandem kites (those in which several
   kites are flown on one line) are classified as belonging to the division
   to which their separate units belong.

ENTRY REQUIREMENTS

It is usually stipulated that all kites must fly, even those which are entered only for judging on the basis of appearance or quality of workmanship. If the judge doubts the airworthiness of a kite, he may require
a demonstration before judging it.

Jacksonville, Florida, allows participants to enter any number of
kites, homemade or purchased, but specifies that only homemade kites
may be entered in the "strongest puller," "best decorated," "most
unique" and "best box kite" contests.

Huntington Park, California, requires that all kites must not only
be handmade, but that they must have a design and a name.

Many communities restrict competition to kites made by the in-
dividuals flying them.

The entrant is usually permitted to have an assistant to help him in
getting the kite into the air; this assistant is sometimes also allowed to
catch the kite as it comes down, but otherwise he may not help the
flyer in any way.

KITES DAY

Sometimes a contest begins with a kite-making race. Contestants are given sticks, paper, string and paste. Down on the ground go the boys and girls to see who can put a kite together fastest.

A race is a race and someone must lose. Perhaps it will be the best kite-maker who has taken time to be particular. Making good kites is a skill, with speed or no speed at all.

TOURNAMENTS

Excitement is sometimes so high that only a stretched rope can hold contestants at a fair line in a race. Winners will be treated like heroes in their communities. The winning kites will be displayed for everyone to admire their flying perfections.

A FEW USUAL EVENTS
100-yard dash for flat kites with tails.
Altitude race for tailless bow kites.
Pulling power contest for box kites.

RIBBON AWARDS are usually for:
Best workmanship.
The highest flyer.
The largest kite.
The smallest kite.
The most beautiful.
The most comical.
The best invention.

ALL IN THE GAME

Kite flying has been compared to going fishing—lots of mishaps, lots of losses, but still lots of fun.

To have your kite damaged is only an interesting obstacle in the game. It can give you the pleasure of using ingenuity in mending it. Or just leave your kite in a tree for next year's birds to nest in, for you know how to make a new and perhaps a better one.

PHOTOGRAPHS IN THIS BOOK